Ida and the Three Visitors

The Historical
Series of the Reformed
Church in America

By Eric & Meredith Schrotenboer

Illustrations By Tyson Ranes

For Meryn and Judah
Mom and Dad

For my cherished family
Tyson

© 2025 Reformed Church Press
All rights reserved. No part of this publication may be reproduced, stored in a retrieval sys-tem, or transmitted in any form or by any means electronic, mechanical, photocopying, re-cording or otherwise, without the prior written permission of the publisher.

Published by Reformed Church Press | Grand Rapids, Michigan
Publisher's Cataloging-in-Publication Data Schrotenboer, Eric.

Ida and the three visitors: the true story of missionary Ida Scudder / Eric and Meredith Schrotenboer ; illustrations by Tyson Ranes. – Grand Rapids, MI : Historical Series of the Reformed Church in America, 2025. p. ; cm.

ISBN13: 978-1-950572-34-2

Scudder, Ida Sophia, 1870-1960. 2. Missionaries, Medical--India—Biography. 3. Women physi-cians--India. I. Title. II. Schrotenboer, Meredith. III. Ranes, Tyson. BV3269.S356 S37 2025 266--dc23

Illustrations: Tyson Ranes
Editor: Glenys Nellist
Design: Mariah Scott
RCA Content Coordinator: Kelli Gilmore

Printed in the United States of America

29 28 27 26 25 • 5 4 3 2 1

Hello! My name is Ida Scudder, and I never wanted to be missionary.

A missionary is someone who shares God's love through their actions and words. Sounds exciting, right?

Well, not to me.

I was born in India, a land bursting with color, bustling markets, and beautiful people. It was a place of endless wonder.

But...

"Ida," my mother would say, "will you help me feed these children? Food has been hard to find, and they are so hungry."

I handed out food with my five older brothers. But it made me feel sad. Why did I always have enough to eat but others didn't?

How could I really make a difference?

I often dreamed about living in America, far away from India.

My new home was on a farm in Nebraska. I loved riding my horse through the wide-open fields and breathing the fresh country air.

But the time came when my parents decided to return to India.

I didn't want to go back.
I didn't want to be a missionary.

And I loved making my friends laugh!

I had made up my mind—I was *not* going to be a missionary. And I was *not* going back to India.

But an unexpected telegram changed everything.

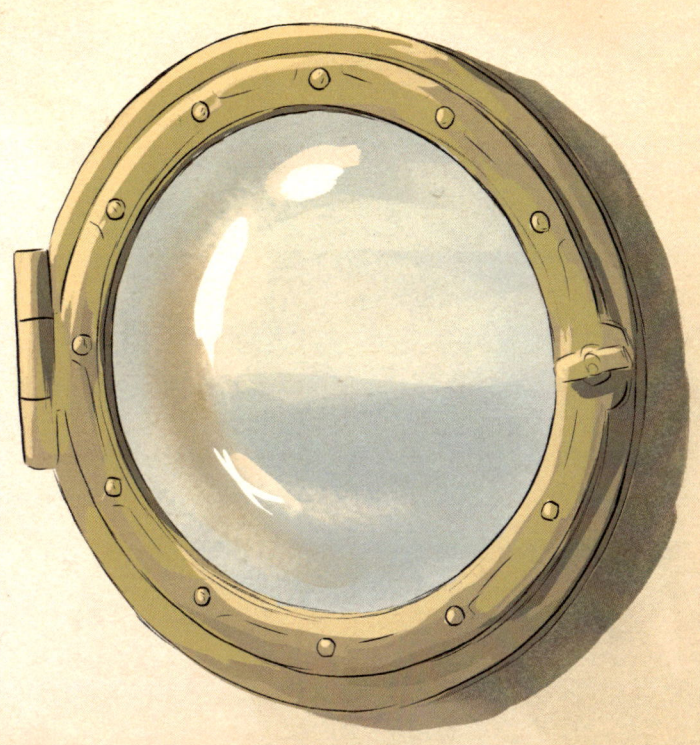

So I packed my bags and sailed back to India.

In India, the sights, sounds, and smells rushed to meet me once again.

And so did the feeling of helplessness. The sick, the hungry, and the poor were still there.

I cared for my mother,

helped with chores at my parent's mission school,

and traveled with my father, giving medical care and teaching about Jesus.

As my mother recovered, we spent many afternoons sipping tea on the porch. I was grateful for those times together...

but I *really* wanted to go back to America—
where no one needed my help.

Then everything changed.

One evening, I heard footsteps and a knock on our front door.
An important Hindu man called a Brahmin bowed before me.

"May I help you?" I asked.

"Yes," he said. "My wife is giving birth to our child, and she needs help. I heard you came from America, and I thought you could help her."

"I'm not a doctor," I said. "I can't help her. But my father can. He's a doctor and he will help your wife."

But the man shook his head. "I believe that another man cannot see my wife like this, even if he is a doctor."

He disappeared into the night.

Later, I heard more footsteps and another knock on the door. Hoping the Brahmin had returned, I opened the door to someone else.

"Salaam, Madam," he said. "May Allah grant you peace." This time, it was a Muslim man with the same request.

"My wife is having our baby and needs your help." So I turned to get my father.

Once again, the man shook his head. "A man cannot enter the room of a woman. Only her husband can."

He bowed and left.

"Sorry to bother you," he said, and sadly walked home.

I couldn't sleep, thinking about the three women who needed help that night. But I wasn't a doctor, and there wasn't a female doctor in the village. How could I really make a difference? I felt helpless.

But in the morning, I knew I could do something.

I prayed.

"God, if You want me to, I will spend my life in India helping women who need care."

With the help of the Women's Board of Foreign Missions, I raised enough money to study at the Women's Medical College of Philadelphia.

When Cornell Medical College in New York City began accepting women, I studied there and graduated with their first class of women doctors.

I knew that God had big plans for me. I was asked to build a hospital to care for women in Vellore, India.

Two years later, we opened that hospital for women in Vellore. It was called the Mary Taber Schell Hospital.

I worked at the hospital, traveled to villages, set up roadside clinics, and helped those who needed care.

We opened a nursing school and a medical college that trained women how to be nurses and doctors.

This college became the Christian Medical College, producing some of the best doctors, surgeons, and scientists in all of India.

Just like God had a plan for my life, God has a plan for your life.

God is preparing YOU for something only YOU can do. When you see someone who needs help, be brave and act!

When you show God's love by what you do and say, YOU are a missionary too!

1898
Ida transfers to and graduates from Cornell Medical School.

1909
Ida starts a school of nursing in Vellore.

1960
Ida Scudder dies in Kodaikanal, India.

1902
The Mary Taber Schell Memorial Hospital for women opens in Vellore, India.

1918
Ida establishes the Missionary Medical School for Women.

1945
Missionary Medical College is renamed Christian Medical College.

1900
Ida returns to India and opens a health clinic in her home.

1947
Christian Medical College begins admitting male students.

1895
Ida begins her medical studies at the Women's Medical College of Philadelphia.

for Parents

Glossary:
Hindu – a believer in the religion of Hinduism.
Brahmin – in Hinduism, a member of the highest class, spiritually and socially.
Muslim – a believer in the religion of Islam.

Ida Scudder died in 1960 at the age of 89, after dedicating her life to serving the community of Vellore, India, and providing compassionate, high-quality healthcare for people from all walks of life. Her tireless efforts and medical legacy continue to inspire hundreds of thousands around the world.

Christian Medical College (CMC) in Vellore, founded through her vision, has gained global recognition for its achievements in medicine. Their contributions include controlling plague outbreaks, rehabilitating leprosy patients, playing a key role in eradicating polio and managing HIV/AIDS. CMC's contributions to public health have had a lasting impact, not just in India but worldwide.

Ida recognized a pressing need and chose to meet it with love and compassion. Her actions demonstrated God's love, and earned her the opportunity to share the message of Jesus with others.

As we share Ida's story with children, it's essential they understand that anyone can be a missionary. God is always at work in the world, and each of us is invited to participate. Some may be called to distant places, while others are called to show God's love to neighbors, friends, and classmates.

Fredrick Buechner once said, "The place God calls you to is the place where your deep gladness and the world's deep hunger meet." This was true for Ida, and it can be true for us. Spend time talking with the children in your life about the needs they see around them and brainstorm together how they can help. We are all missionaries, and God desires to use each of us, no matter our age, to make a difference in the world.

Discussion Questions:

1. Missionaries are people who show God's love through their words and actions.
Who can be a missionary?

2. Sometimes sharing God's love with others begins with noticing the needs around you.
What needs do you see?

3. Do you have an idea of how to help meet one of those needs?

4. How might we meet those needs together?

5. What is our first step?

Sources

Benge, Janet, and Geoff Benge. *Ida Scudder: Healing Bodies, Touching Hearts (Christian Heroes: Then and Now)*. YWAM Publishing, 2005.

Wilson, Dorothy Clark. *Dr. Ida*. McGraw-Hill, 1959.

Kelly, Terri B. *Ida Scudder: Missionary Doctor*. BJU Press, 2021.

www.ingramcontent.com/pod-product-compliance
Lightning Source LLC
Chambersburg PA
CBRC090911230426
43673CB00018B/426